Conversations with Wisdom

Conversations with Wisdom

Spiritual Treasures I and II

LeXuan Tran Koss

VANTAGE PRESS
New York

Conversations with Wisdom: Spiritual Treasures I and II, is dedicated to His Holiness, Pope John Paul II and his Papacy. This dedication is a thank-you for his continual prayers said for me during the years spent in completing these spiritual writings. The Holy Father truly has been to me and to the flock of Jesus Christ, a "Light" to the world.

This book is also dedicated to His Excellency, Cardinal Francis Xavier Nguyen Van Thuan, President of the Pontifical Council of Justice and Peace.

SECRETARIAT OF STATE

Dear Ms. Tran,

His Holiness Pope John Paul II has directed me to acknowledge the kind letter and enclosures which you sent to him.

His Holiness appreciates the sentiments which prompted this devoted gesture and he invokes upon you the peace and joy of our Lord Jesus Christ. I also have the honor to convey his Apostolic Blessing.

Sincerely yours,

Monsignor G.B. Re
Assessor

SECRETARIAT OF STATE

FROM THE VATICAN. August 26, 1985

Dear Ms. Tran,

    His Holiness Pope John Paul II has directed me
to acknowledge the kind letter and the two books
which you sent to him.

    His Holiness appreciates the sentiments which
prompted this devoted gesture, and he invokes upon
you the peace and joy of our Lord Jesus Christ. I
also have the honor to convey his Apostolic Blessing.

Sincerely yours,

Monsignor R. Marsiglio
Department Head

SECRETARIAT OF STATE

Dear Ms. Thi Tran,

    His Holiness Pope John Paul II duly received your letter and typescript and he has directed me to send you this acknowledgment. He appreciates the sentiments which prompted you to share your thoughts with him.

    His Holiness is pleased to assure you of a remembrance in his prayers, and he invokes upon you God's blessings.

Sincerely yours,

O. Rizzato

Monsignor O. Rizzato
Department Head

SECRETARIAT OF STATE

——

FIRST SECTION · GENERAL AFFAIRS

FROM THE VATICAN,

December 9, 1993

Dear LeXuan,

The Holy Father has received your letter, and he has directed me to reply in his name.

His Holiness wishes me to assure you that he is praying for you and the members of your prayer group.

He invokes upon all of you God's blessings of grace and peace.

Sincerely yours,

Monsignor L. Sandri
Assessor

LeXuan Tran Koss
1250 North Stephora Avenue
Covina, CA 91724

SECRETARIAT OF STATE
—
FIRST SECTION · GENERAL AFFAIRS

From the Vatican, November 26, 1996

Dear Mrs. Koss,

The Holy Father has asked me to thank you for your letter and gift of two books. He is very appreciative of your thoughtful gesture and of the devoted sentiments it manifests.

His Holiness invokes upon you the grace and peace of God our Father and of our Lord Jesus Christ.

Sincerely yours,

Monsignor L. Sandri
Assessor

Mrs. LeXuan Tran Koss
1250 North Stephora Avenue
Covina, CA 91 724

J. M. ✠ J. T.

May 16, 1985

Dear Le Xuan,

    I really enjoyed reading your spiritual writings. Thank you kindly for sharing them with me and my Carmelite family. Your writings express a true and genuine love for Our Lord and our Blessed Lady which I know God will put to use for the good of many souls.

    People can often forget by looking for God in extraordinary ways that His love can be found in the simplicity and humility of a grateful heart. The spirit of your writings beautifully reflect these qualities.

    I will pray very specially for you to our Lady during her month of May asking her to make you her instrument through which Christ's love will always shine. May she always keep you near her loving and pure heart.

                  In Christ's love,
                  Sister Emma Luz, O.C.D.

BLESSED SACRAMENT COMMUNITY
SAINT JOSEPH'S RECTORY
352 SOUTH MAIN STREET
OLD TOWN, MAINE 04468
TELEPHONE: 827-7741

MARCH 10, 1986

MY DEAREST LEXUAN

MANY AND SINCERE THANKS AGAIN FOR YOUR LETTER AND ENCLOSURE OF 2-22-86.
THE GOOD LORD BLESS YOU AND YOUR GENUINE ENDEAVORS. I SEE THAT YOU ALSO HAVE TO FACE SO
MANY TRIALS AND OPPOSITIONS. OUR DEAR LORD JESUS ALSO MET WITH SO MUCH OF THIS, AND HE
SAID THAT WE, HIS FOLLOWERS, COULD ALSO EXPECT THE SAME KIND OF TREATMENT, DIDN'T HE?
BUT WE KEEP UP OUR TRUST AND FAITH THAT WE ALSO WITH HIM WILL TRIUMPH FOR GOD'S GREATER
GLORY. MY PRAYERS AND MY LOVE GO WITH YOU ALWAYS.

AS REGARDS THE HOME FOR THE UNFORTUNATE MY ADVICE IS FOR YOU TO LINK UP WITH THE
SISTERS OF MOTHER THERESA OF CULCUTA. THEY ARE MANY, HEROIC, AND SO EFFICIENT. OK?
GOD BLESS AND KEEP YOU, MY DEAREST LEXUAN. LOVE AND PRAYERS, YOUR PADRECITO

J. Roberge s.s.s.

Contents

Foreword

Our need in the present moment of our history, at the turn of the millennium, to listen to the Lord and attend His Word, has never been greater or more critical. With the enormous advances and expansion of technology throughout every level of our lives and throughout the world, the old boundaries of culture and identity by which we marked out who we were in the world and where we belonged in it, and which gave meaning to our lives, are now being radically replaced by a global culture, with ever broadening horizons of information and widening social possibilities. The old touchstones of shared values and views that bring us coherence as we live in our own corner of the world provide less certitude as the world shrinks and alternative points of view overwhelm us.

As Catholics, our Church is that secure place from which we can respond to this overwhelming onslaught of endless possibilities and countless opinions, which clamor for priority. In Tradition and Scripture, we have the guide we need for the choices we are challenged to make. But these do not operate automatically. And given the turbulence of ideas and experiences that surround us, we are even more in need of learning how to attend to them with greater care and faith. It is prayer that must teach us how.

The Lord of Light Prayer Group has been meeting for over seven years in simple response to the Spirit's invitation to "be still and know that I am God." I have been privileged to have been for a time the Spiritual Director and to remain in close touch with LeXuan Tran Koss, who, with her husband, Larry, and two sons, John and Daniel, opens her home for the group to meet. LeXuan receives allocutions and though these have neither been formally investigated nor authenticated by the Church, they have proved a source of personal inspiration to LeXuan, and of great edification for the group as she made them known.

Though as a priest of the Archdiocese of Los Angeles, I must reserve any official opinion concerning them. LeXuan's intimate experience of God has been a sure example and constant call to all in the group to greater prayer and a more quiet listening to the Word, who speaks best to us in the silence of obedience and willing hearts. The words of this book, *Conversations with Wisdom, Spiritual Treasures I & II*, were heard in such a heart.

May we all, surrounded as we are, by the cacophony of a world filled with voices all claiming our attention, learn quiet listening to the Word that LeXuan shares with us in this book.

Father Eugene Herbert
1 November 1999
Solemnity of All Saints

Preface

Why This Book

To provide you, the young and elderly, rich and poor, fortunate and unfortunate, with an understanding to troublesome questions that at times can lead us from God, or can lead us to God.

An understanding was provided to the author over a sixteen year period to questions such as: does God love me; do I need God's help; who really is my enemy; what is faith; why my sufferings; why the rich and the poor; why do we have problems; why do we have to forgive; why do we need to pray; what prayer is most pleasing to God; where is God found; how to be one with the Lord?

An understanding to these questions leads to responding to Jesus' request, "Learn of Me."

Introduction

Conversations with Wisdom: Spiritual Treasures I is a collection of spiritual writings on wisdom that were written in my single state as LeXuan Thi Tran, from 1984 through 1986. During that time, I was blind. I had been blind since 1978.

Conversations with Wisdom: Spiritual Treasures II was done in my married state, 1990–2000, after my eyesight had been partially restored in December 1989.

Mainly the writings are done in a style used long ago in the early stages of Christianity, the use of dialogues. This is a communication of question and answer between an inquirer and a responder.

Why are these writings on wisdom Spiritual Treasures? They are to give hope to those who are handicapped, hope to those in suffering, hope to those in darkness, and strength to those in light to persevere and stay close to Jesus and Mary.

You see, I was in darkness, physical and spiritual. I trusted in the Lord and Mary, but why me, O Lord? Now I know why. This is explained in chapter 21 of this book, "I Am Now One with the Lord," which was recently completed.

In 1978, a sickness struck me down, Cryptococcal Meningitis. The doctors didn't give me too much of a chance to live. A Vietnamese Redemptionist Priest gave a picture to my family who placed it, the Mother of Perpetual Help, over my bed. From that time on, a recovery took place without a medical answer being given.

Just prior to the entrance into the hospital, my sight was lost.

A story that is now known resulted from this. I forgave the doctor, accepted God's will, and with my sight handicap went to college.

In August 1983, after a person met me providentially after Mass, God's plan for me started to unfold. Through the friendship of this person, *Spiritual Treasures I* was made possible. *Spiritual Treasures I* could never have evolved without first my loss of sight, spending almost one year in a hospital and going to college. God's ways are inscrutable and mysterious. All He wants is for us to do His Will. Peace to those who benefit from these writings on wisdom.

LeXuan Thi Tran Koss

Acknowledgments

A very special thank you to Ms. Holly Hargis for her diligence and perseverance in putting into type the Spiritual Treasure writings. Also to my loving husband, who proofread and did the logistics for the writings, and even had the foresight to make copies of the originals, which by doing so, he protected the writings from being lost.

Yes, I gave into temptation and destroyed the original writings, believing they were of no value. Why would God choose to have a dialogue with one who could not see, had little faith, and even believed God was up there and not down here?

However, "My soul. I chose you to do My will. Go now and My Peace be with you. Do not fear to teach others what I have taught you."

"Yes, Lord, I am your servant. Let it be done to me according to Your Word."

The cover is a symbolic representation of a vision given to me relating to a mission of the "Lord of Light" prayer group, of which I am the representative.

The vision, as shown on the cover, was done by James K. Duke.

Declaration

In response to the advice of a fervent Catholic friend, the following declaration is made:

In accordance with the decrees of the Catholic Church, the author declares that only private and human faith is attributed to the words in these spiritual writings, especially in the portions containing dialogue. Extraordinary graces and incidence are related in these writings to which The Church has not yet added its decrees of approval.

Furthermore, the author has no intention of anticipating the judgment of the Holy See, to which she willingly and entirely submits herself.

SPIRITUAL TREASURES I

1.

A Holy Man, Servant of the Lord

This writing is so loved by children, it is suggested those in the CCD program might consider it for a play.

In December, 1984, the Feast of the Immaculate Conception, this writing was sent as a gift to His Holiness, Pope John Paul II. His Apostolic blessing was later received.

Who was the man that needed help? The answer always brings love and joy to hearts of all ages.

Mr. K is a very poor man. He does not have anything to offer the world but the love of his heart. He loves his God and his neighbors. The sad thing is his neighbors reject him. They throw him down on the ground and step all over him because of the four-letter word P O O R. What a life for Mr. K!

One day, Mr. K goes to see his friend because he wants to know if his friend can help him. On the way to his friend's house, he meets a man. The man needs help because he can hardly walk on his feet. Mr. K wants to help him, but he fears. Mr. K says to himself, *"If I try to help him, he will refuse because that man seems like a rich man and I am so opposite of him."*

Mr. K wants to walk away from this man, but his heart does not allow him to leave. So he slowly walks toward the rich man and politely says, "Do you need any help, sir? If you do, may I help you, sir?" The rich man begins to tell Mr. K what happened to him and he asks Mr. K to take him home in Mr. K's car.

On the way home, the rich man asks Mr. K, "What are you doing for a living?" Mr. K tells the rich man the truth, that he has not been working, and he has a hard time finding work. The rich man tells Mr. K not to worry about it, and he offers Mr. K a job. Mr. K is happy to obtain work again. The rich man tells him, "If you work for me, you have to do whatever I ask you to do." Mr. K responds, "Yes, sir. And please tell me what kind of job that you want me to do."

The rich man shook his head. "Wait for me a moment, my son, I have not finished yet. Listen! If you would like to work for me, first you must give yourself to me."

"I don't understand, sir."

"My son, what don't you understand? It is so simple. I just want you to give me your mind, eyes, ears, tongue, hands and feet."

Mr. K looks at the rich man in disbelief and speaks with concern in his voice. "Sir, I don't know what you are talking about, but if I give you everything, then how can I work for you? Why don't you ask me to give you the rest of myself, like my heart and my—"

"My son, you still do not understand, do you? I am glad that you mentioned your heart. Why not? Of course, I also ask you to give your heart to me."

Mr. K's eyes are wide open. He does not know what the rich man is up to. Suddenly he feels someone touch his shoulder and he feels warm. He says to himself, "Is this from the rich man's hand? It can't be."

The rich man smiles and says to Mr. K, "I knew you would not understand, but don't worry. I am going to explain to you now."

"Yes, I think you better."

4

The rich man begins. "My son, answer me. What makes a human being be alive?"

"I think the heart, sir."

"You said, you think the heart. Why does it have to be the heart, my son?"

"The heart is what helps human beings to be alive, because the heart helps to circulate the blood. And if the heart stops, then the human being also stops living."

"So what is this telling you?"

Mr. K says out loud, "I would say that if human beings need the heart for the center of their lives, they also need love for themselves, too. To give life, love to others."

The rich man shook his head. "Yes, to love one another is life. *(The rich man continues.)* In order for you to work for me, you must trust in me completely. You should not doubt about me. You must give your mind to me because I will help you to think of me when you are in trouble. You must give your eyes to me, then I can guide you to go my way and see things that you haven't seen before. You also must give your ears that I will help you to listen well when your friends call you for help. You must give your hand to me that I will help you to write. You also must give me your feet, then I will guide you to walk my way. Finally, the last thing I want to have is your tongue because I will speak for you. Do not be afraid, my son. I will be with you. From now on, you are my servant. Peace, my son!"

Mr. K stops his car and looks to the right. The rich man is not there. Mr. K closes his eyes and says, "O God, You are my God."

Note:

This was a writing in symbols about Mr. K to bring forth his merits to others and protect his identity. Yes, he is living.

2.

The Cat and the Bird

Who is the cat, the bird, and what does the cage represent? When you find out, it is hoped you can share the answer with others.

The Lord

Soul, let me tell you the story about the cat and the bird.

Soul

Yes, Lord, please do so.

The Lord

Once there was a beautiful white bird. It was spotless. There was nothing to change its beauty. There was also a big black cat, which wanted so much to stain the whiteness of the bird. The cat then made a plan to get the white bird. The cat began to play around the cage where the beautiful white bird was staying. The bird was able always to protect its whiteness because the cage was up where the black cat could not reach it.

Then it happened. The cage fell where the black cat could now reach it. The impact of the fall opened the door of the cage. At this moment, the black cat put its paw into the cage and struck the bird. The cat then played around in victory thinking the bird was helpless. Then the cat swallowed the bird.

Soul

Lord, why are You telling me this? The story that You told has nothing to do with me. It is only about a cat eating a bird, nothing else.

The Lord

Wait my soul, I knew that you would not be able to understand. Therefore I am here to teach you because of my love for you.

Soul

O yes, O God, You are my God. Please teach me so I know the meaning of this story to bring Your light to others.

The Lord

In this story, I used the beautiful white bird to indicate the beauty of your soul, which I have given to you. This beauty can be kept with the help of my grace through my Mother, Mary. The cage, which I mentioned, represents your body. The body is very easy to penetrate but it can only be penetrated through its door, the will, which is the door of the cage. Only you can open or close this door. The whiteness is then under your control with its security being my grace. Soul, please answer me this question. Who do you think the cat is?

Soul

Lord, it is the devil, his darkness, vices, and his temptations.

The Lord

Yes, my soul, you are right. Only with My Light could you have answered this properly. What does this mean to you now?

Soul

Your kingdom is found within. It is whiteness, virtue. It can be kept, within the body only with Your help, grace, and through Your Mother, Mary.

The cage can fall, but if we remember to call upon You or Your Blessed Mother, Mary, we will be helped by Your grace, Your seven Sacraments. Then our whiteness will return; the cat will reject us and find out that we are not helpless. The victory is Yours and the cat, which is Satan, loses. Lord, please save me!

The Lord

Do not fear. I will be with you always. My soul, I give my peace to you.

Soul

Lord, I am not worthy to receive You. But only say the word, and I shall be healed.

May 31, 1985
Feast of Visitation

3.

Three Fingers

Where is God's house? The importance of prayer and love. Three fingers are used as symbols to relate to the family and Holy Trinity. Please read on.

Soul

*(calling out)*Lord, I am weary of looking for You. Where are You? I want to adore and worship You, but I don't know where You are!

The Lord

Soul, you have found Me. I am always with you. Why are you upset?

Soul

Lord. How? And what do you mean when You say that You are always with me?

The Lord

I teach you this for you to give to others. You have to fully understand that My Home is within you. My Kingdom is a Kingdom of Hearts, and I am the King. My Mother and yours, Our Blessed Mary Ever Virgin, is the Queen.

Also, you should understand the importance of prayer and talking about My Kingdom, for wherever two or more are gathered together in My Name, there I Am.

Soul

O Lord. Thank you. Please, please teach me more. I am so hungry to hear Your Words.

The Lord

Love is life. Every thing is based on love. God the Father, the Creator out of love, created the world, man, and sent Me, His Only Begotten Son, to save man from eternal death. With this in mind, how can man solve problems related to love, happiness, and peace?

Soul

Lord, I am so excited. The answer is love. Love is life. What we give we receive.

The Lord

Yes. Love. God is Love. God is Life. This love can only be found in the family, established as the foundation. Like My

Love, God is Love, is the foundation of My Church. Oh, what blessings man receives from above.

The family can be thought in terms like the Holy Trinity. It is based on love as the foundation. One in Three. Three in One. That is love proceeds from the husband and the wife, the result being a child. The Holy Spirit coming forth as a separate Person from the Love of the Father and the Son.

Look at your hand. Look at your inner three fingers. Are they not formed together like one at the base of the hand? The middle seems to be the strength of the two surrounding it, like it came forth from the other two's mutual need for help, love. Like the child of the family. The parents, needing an expression, a visible sign of their love for strength to go on.

Remember I gave to you the Holy Spirit as your Strengthener, Consoler in time of need.

Soul

Lord, Your use of the fingers for having a thought better understood is like the one used before to describe a good way to remember the Ten Commandments You gave us. The ten fingers, each one representing a commandment, with each thumb representing Love, the basis of the commandments, Love of God and Love of neighbor.

The Lord

Soul, you are so full of My Light and Grace to respond as well as you are doing. Blessed are you.

Soul

O God, You Are My God. The more You say, the more I want to hear. I don't believe I have found such a treasure. A treasure of Love. Your Wisdom. But, O Lord, I have a question. How do you love a person when a person hurts you?

The Lord

My soul, you have to learn to forgive as I forgave. Also pray for those who hurt you. With My Grace nothing is impossible. I know this is not easy for you. That is why you need Me in your life because humility is understanding that you completely depend on Me.

Soul

Oh, yes, Lord, You are right. I am sorry. Is there anything else that You want me to share with others?

The Lord

My soul, this you must understand is important for you to know how to use the knowledge like keys to enter My Kingdom. Especially to keep My Commandments relating to marriage, abortion, and love of God and your neighbor, family. My Commandments are the strength for society, the family and My Church. Mankind and society will fare well only with Me. Go now and My Peace be with you. Do not fear to teach others what I have taught you.

Soul

My heart wants to sing a song. You are Beautiful, O Lord. Love is the center of our life. If there is no love it seems like the sun is not shining. Without You, there is no happiness. Without You, the birds stop singing; without You, the wind will not blow. Without You, there are no stars or moon in the sky. Everything is death. Please, O Lord, come back soon to share Your Love.

June 8, 1985
Feast of St. Michael
of the Saints, Trinitarian

4.

The Lord of Light

God does not abandon you, but you can leave Him. Why?

The Lord

Come, come to Me, my soul! My favorite delight.
     At our last visit you asked me to please come back soon, your request is now granted. You are my delight. I could not wait any longer.

Soul

Lord. Yes, Lord Jesus Christ. I know You are here. I now come to You. I give to You my attention. I am thirsting to hear Your Words, receive Your Light.

The Lord

Soul, tell me, what do you see in front of you?

Soul

Lord, I see three trees in front of me. One tree is dry, it seems that it is going to die. Another tree has a lot of thorns around it, and the third is beautiful. It is a big tree with a lot of fruits. Lord, why do You ask me this?

The Lord

The reason is that it is like the last time I visited you, to use things visible to you to help you understand My Kingdom. By this understanding it is then easier to teach others as I have taught you, especially about good and evil.

Soul

I understand, O Lord. Please forgive me for asking. I remember Your Words of request, "Learn of Me." Yes, Lord, I am ready to hear about the three trees. Please go on about good and evil.

The Lord

Soul, look at the dried tree and tell me why it is dried, near death?

Soul

Lord, the tree is dried because there is no one to take care of it.

The Lord

You are right, my soul. The tree is dried because there is no one to take care of it. It is the same way with the human being. People forget what I have given to them.

I have given to each a heart to love Me, My Kingdom, and their neighbor. I have also given to each a soul, which needs caring because eternal life or death depends on care given. They do not take care of their hearts, love, their soul, grace. They only run after worldly, material things.

Soul, do you understand what I am teaching you? Remember what you wrote in one of your writings about My Kingdom. "Faith without works is dead."

Soul

Lord, I think You want to teach me that we have to take care of our souls as well as material things. We do good and avoid evil.

The Lord

Yes, that is right. With My grace, Light, you are doing fine. Now tell Me about the tree with the thorns.

Soul

If the tree has thorns and you touch it, it will hurt. Does this tree represent the Devil?

The Lord

I knew that you would be able to understand this. You are right again. It is Satan. He lies in wait for you with his fruits (thorns), poison death. The thorns wait for you. They try to get inside, and when they do they hurt.

They get in through the heart, the will, but they cannot enter into the soul. This is My area alone. They try to tarnish, blemish the soul by robbing it of graces I have given to it and make available to it. But if you water it with My food, the thorns cannot enter or if they are in and pricking you, they will leave.

Soul

Lord, how do we protect ourselves from this happening?

The Lord

By remembering Me by staying away from the tree of pleasure, vice, evils, thorns, the kingdom of evil, praying, especially the Rosary, to ask Mary, the Blessed Mother, to help you; say an "Our Father," a "Hail Mary."

Soul

Lord, how do I teach others the way You are teaching me?

The Lord

Do not worry how to teach others because I will speak through you to others. You do not speak about My Kingdom by yourself. Do not be afraid.

Soul

What a pleasure it is for me to learn about Your Wisdom, Your Kingdom. What joy it brings to me. Please tell me about the third tree, the beautiful one.

The Lord

I don't think I have to. Try to tell me your thoughts.

Soul

The beautiful tree is a soul living in Your grace, being watered, nourished by You, staying close to You and Your Mother, Mary, the fruits being good works, especially love and forgiveness towards our neighbor. The tree is responding to Your grace. It is living in You, and You in the soul in fullness.

The Lord

Oh, my delight. You are ready to go forth to teach others about My Kingdom. You are so right. However, there is one last question. In order for the tree to live, stay beautiful and obtain more fruits, what does it need?

Soul

The tree must need someone to take care of it. Also the tree needs the sun to give it life, water, and fertilizer.

The Lord

Well done. How is this best done?

Soul

You, O Lord. Partaking of Your Body and Blood. Because You have said, "Those who eat My Body and drink My Blood, I live in them and they shall not die."

The Lord

I want to see all My people like the beautiful tree. Growing with Me, suffering with Me, and helping Me in others where the tree is dying or growing. I am a God of Mercy. I thirst for souls. Please help Me and pray for others to come to Me like you have by responding to My Grace.

Soul

Lord, I don't know what to do without You.

The Lord

Peace be with you. Now go and teach others.

Soul

Yes, Lord. I am Your servant. Let it be done to me according to Your Word.

June 11, 1985
Feast of St. Barnabas, Apostle
2:30 A.M.—4:20 A.M.

5.

Lord, You Know Best

Problems occur; we blame the Lord, but in the end, we are a better person for having gone through the trial. This is another writing in a series of writings, written to uplift hearts to God and provide light and hope to those in need.

Soul

Lord, the more I think of You, the more I am upset with You. Lord, do You know how upset I am towards You?

The Lord

My soul, I know you much more than you know Me, and I love you much more than you love Me.

Soul

Lord, You have said to me that You know me more than I know You and You love me much more than I love You. That is not right. I think it is the opposite way.

The Lord

It is all right. You said that you love Me much more than I love you. Now you tell Me how.

Soul

This is how, O Lord. I have done a lot for You as You have asked me to. You asked me to:

1. Forgive a certain person and also apologize.
2. To return something that meant so much to me.
3. To accept and agree to marry the same person I was to forgive.

Then, besides all of these, You asked me to trust in You and this person, which I have not doubted in all sincerity to do. I have done this because I know that You visit me at Your choosing, and when You do so, You ask me things that others would hesitate in doing. But why, Lord? Why have You made me this way? Why am I so suffering? Lord, don't You see my heart is bleeding? Lord, don't You see how much that I love You, and how this love is bringing pain to me?

The Lord

Are you finished now, my soul, in opening up your heart to Me? If you are, then please now listen to Me. My soul, I ask you this question: Who died on the cross for you? Answer Me.

Soul

Yes, O Lord. You did. When one gets upset, things cannot be seen as You see them.

The Lord

Do you know how sorrowful I am? I love all of My people. I give them everything that they need to live on this earth, and I died for their sins. But the sorrow is My people turn away from Me. How painful I am now because when things go wrong, my people always blame Me that I don't love them enough, the sign being that they have problems.

Soul

Lord, I am sorry I hurt You. Lord, I ask You to forgive. Also, I am sorry others hurt You. Lord, You know best.

The Lord

My soul, do not worry because I forgive you for all the things that you said earlier. I am a patient, merciful, and understanding God *(The Lord then stops for a while)*. My soul, do you know why your heart is bleeding?

Soul

My Lord, I am not sure if I do.

The Lord

I know that you do not understand; that is why I asked you, why I am here. I died on the Cross because of man's sins, to redeem him.

I give man and my people a piece of that Cross to carry. The piece of the Cross that I give to each of you depends on each individual whether light or heavy. But I never give you more than you can carry.

The sad point is that my children do not understand this and they get upset at Me quickly for what is happening to them. They do not understand that by doing this they are being trapped by Satan.

Remember My life and My family. Did we have problems? All problems are permitted by My Father to test you and to help lead you and others to your eternal home. Satan knows this and when problems occur, he tries quickly to get you angry and upset at God so you think God doesn't love you and you will leave Him to follow Satan, the powerful and wealthy of the world. They can help you, but God can't because He doesn't love you any more.

Do you remember when I was dying on the Cross, I said, "My God, My God, why hast thou forsaken Me?" But I didn't leave My Father. I then said, "I commend My Spirit into Thy Hands." My Father didn't abandon Me. He then raised Me up on the third day. Now I am beside you.

If my people could only be patient and think of what is in the Bible, Words of Wisdom, Understanding, Knowledge, Light, and Love as well as examples of what happened to others, especially My people. This is a weakness of My people and of mankind. They forget what I have given to them to help them when in need. This is why your heart is bleeding. You do not turn to Me enough by finding Me in helps I have given to You.

Helps especially like My Mother, Mary. Remember I also have said "Pray Always."

Soul

O Lord, how impressive. Oh, how wonderful to hear You say this, to explain this to me. O Lord, thank you, thank you so much that You opened my eyes to see the truth. I understand clearly and perfectly now. When we are weak, in trouble, we get strong by seeking strength in You and in this way stay close to You.

How can man ever doubt in Your ways, O Lord? Thanks be to God. Yes, O Lord, I am a better person for having gone through difficulties given by Your Divine Wisdom.

The Lord

Peace be with you.

Soul

O God, You are my God. Please come back soon, for I look forward to learning more from You. In my joy, I wish to now say the beautiful prayer of consecration to You that is part of my people's devotion in our prayer form to the Mother of Perpetual Help.

July 14, 1985
Feast of St. Camillus De Lellis
4:30 P.M.–6:28 P.M.

Consecration

O Lord Jesus Christ,

> I give You my mind, to think of You;
> I give You my eyes, to see as You see;
> I give You my ears, to hear Your Word;
> I give You my tongue, to speak of You;
> I give You my heart, to grow to love You;
> I give You my hands, to do Your work;
> I give You my feet, to go Your way;

O Lord Jesus Christ, I love, I love You so much, so that I will give myself to You, so that You can live, work, and pray in me.

Amen.

6.
Lord, Why My Sufferings?

Over time, problems, sufferings occur. Why? Why me?

Soul

O Lord, please come to me. My heart is troubling. Please come.

The Lord

Yes, my soul. Are you calling Me?

Soul

Oh, yes, Lord. You are my Lord. I am so happy to see You again.

The Lord

All right, my soul. What is troubling you?

Soul

Lord, the last time You came, You brought Light to me about problems. Could You help me to now understand why I had such a serious sickness that I almost died, and why I lost my sight? O Lord, a person can get so disappointed with You when these sufferings occur. You know what is best for us, but why did You give me such a heavy Cross? I love You so much, but You must love me even more because of these special sufferings given.

The Lord

Is that all that is troubling you?

Soul

Lord, the sufferings were so difficult to bear, why didn't You take me away from this earth? What did I do wrong to be given them?

The Lord

My Soul, you will be given Light to help you understand about your sufferings. There are three kinds of sufferings: 1. Direct punishment from sin one commits; 2. Chastisement to help one to seek repentance from things they are doing wrong or have done wrong; 3. For greater virtue for the soul.

You are in the third area. Now does that help you understand why I then didn't take you away from this earth? Haven't you with the help of My grace overcome these sufferings?

Soul

O Lord, whenever You help me see why something happened, and explain it so simply, joy enters my heart and the suffering is conquered. The suffering is somehow related to feelings in the heart. With this Light and the help of Your grace, I can help others to bear with their sufferings by bringing joy and then peace to their hearts. Oh, what a blessing it is to share in Your Light.

The Lord

My soul, now you can see even more about My Wisdom. When you suffer, and especially when it is overcome, you are then able to be a messenger of mine to help others to better bear their sufferings, crosses, and even maybe help them to be overcome. Now as a reward for your bearing with your crosses, I will provide you with more Light on your two big sufferings.

1. Did you come closer to My Mother in your time of need?

2. Did you change your mind on the vocation you had your heart set on?

3. Were you led to meeting your to be husband?

4. Was he led to you by his charity to help you in your time of need?

5. Have you been protected from physical harm from the wrath of Satan who was trying to destroy you through a member of your family?

6. Have you obtained grace from bearing with your sufferings to now help others through your spiritual writings and example?

7. Have you been exalted by your humility to have been given the grace to forward your writings to My Vicar, Pope John Paul II, and a Cardinal and two Bishops?

Soul

Lord, how can we question You? Yes, all these questions have the same answer, yes.

The Lord

Now that you see better why your sufferings and how you were rewarded for your acceptance of them, I wish to show you how I know what is in your heart, and the hearts of all men. Did you make any promise to My Mother, Mary?

Soul

Yes, O Lord.

The Lord

Did you promise Her that you would say the Rosary and go to daily Mass?

Soul

Yes, O Lord. I also said that if I missed Mass one day, I would receive any punishment from Your Mother, Mary.

The Lord

Have you done what you have promised My Mother, Mary? I know you have devoted your life to Her. However, She has not asked you to promise Her anything except to be good, to do good, to say the Rosary and to honor My Glory. Is it difficult to do?

Soul

O Lord, please forgive me again. I am not trying to defend myself here. But I have to be honest with You because I have so many difficulties in trying to adjust to a new life. Yes, before the major sicknesses, I now know that I spent too much time in my studies and didn't spend any time with You and Your Mother, Mary, or anyone else. I now see that when I was in the hospital, I had time to think of You, Your Ways, and call on Your Mother for continuous help.

The Lord

Yes, my soul, you are right. My Mother, Mary, wanted you to review yourself again and to build you up with My Light, the Light of God. You mentioned you called Her name continuously while in the hospital and if you could only know what graces came to your soul by doing so.

A good example is remember when you had such terrible chills and had such pain in your head that you called out loud, "Mother, please help me!! Help me, Mother." During that time, the doctor had covered you with eight thick blankets and you were still cold. The doctor then asked one of the nurses to find some more blankets while he went to get some medicine for your headache. Then as soon as they left the room, you slept in peace. When they came back with the blankets and medicine, they were full of surprise to see you no longer in chill or with pain, or in tears.

Yes, my soul, my delight, you were suffering for the sins of others, you, as I told earlier, are my true cross.

Soul

Thank you, O Lord.

The Lord

Another example, which you know is the reason you are still alive today, is the time after the blanket incident when the doctors had given you a one percent chance of living. You resigned yourself to acceptance of your sufferings and put your life in the hands of My Mother. The doctor's told the nurses to give you anything that you wanted to eat. You knew that meant that they had given up on your recovery. You didn't; you still had hope in Me and My Mother. You know then what miraculously happened.

Soul

Yes, O Lord. A Vietnamese Redemptorist Priest gave to my family to give to me a picture of the Mother of Perpetual Help and received permission to have it placed over my hospital bed. Soon after, I started to recover. The doctors then found out why I was sick. O Lord, why do You and Your Mother love me and others so much when I offend You so much?

The Lord

Now you know more of My immense love for souls.

Soul

Lord, I am not worthy to receive You, but only say the word and I shall be healed. Yes, O Lord, I have believed that You and Your Blessed Mother, Mary, have watched over me. Yes, as the Blessed Mother has said, "I always watch over my children."

7.

Lord, Open My Eyes

The rich and the poor. Why?

Soul

Lord, I need Your help again. I need You to explain a certain way of life to me, the rich and the poor.

The Lord

Soul, I am here. What is it you would like to know about the rich and the poor?

Soul

O Lord, I am so happy to see You again. I have such a problem with the thought of the rich and the poor, it is driving me crazy. Jesus, please teach me and help me to understand why some people are so rich and some people are so poor, and why the rich step on the poor.

Lord, I tell You the truth that I don't like the rich people because of their attitude. They think they are the best and they look down on others, especially towards the poor. In their eyes, everyone is a thief, that is they are always right and others are always wrong, which I don't like. I don't think they trust anyone, including You, O Lord.

The Lord

My soul, My joy and delight, you are so right. I know you are upset as I am, thus I want you to listen carefully. My soul, remember in your writing about, "Lord, Why My Sufferings?" I explained to you people forget to call on Me for help?

Soul

Yes, O Lord.

The Lord

This question you have asked Me about riches, the rich and the poor, relates to why people do call on Me and why in My mercy people are poor. When you are in need, don't you seek help? When in extreme need, don't you usually turn to God?

Soul

Yes, O Lord.

The Lord

When you are in need, don't you listen better?

Soul

Yes, O Lord.

The Lord

Are you now in need? Did you call on Me? Are you now listening? Are you poor?

Soul

Yes, O Lord.

The Lord

I desire all men to be saved. My enemy and yours, Satan, wants all men to be damned, lost, for all eternity with him and his evil spirits in the fires of hell. Do you think that Satan is going to offer you suffering, poverty, wisdom of God, knowledge of God, so you can be with him? No. He wants to offer you riches, power, fame, worldly wisdom, pleasure, activity so you have little opportunity to know, love and serve his greatest and more powerful enemy, God, "I Am Who Am." He does not want you to take time to listen or seek Truth.

In My mercy, I give you what you need. Be content with what you have. Do not be ambitious. Seek ye first the kingdom of God and then all things will be given to thee.

The poor, My soul, have a better chance of finding Me, and staying with Me, and leading others to Me, especially the rich. For when the rich help you, the poor, they help Me. Remember the words of My Mother: "He hath filled the hungry with good things and the rich he hath sent away empty."

Soul

Lord, my eyes are now starting to open. I am now starting to see Your light and wisdom and mercy. Please go on, O Lord.

The Lord

You also have also asked why the rich step on the poor? The answer is simple. Likes go with likes. Do you step on others, or do you respect them and help them? Are you with Me?

Soul

Yes, O Lord.

The Lord

Are the rich usually with Me or against Me? Is Satan with Me or against Me?

Soul

Against You, O Lord.

The Lord

The rich in worldly things, riches, fame, possessions, worldly knowledge, step on their opposites, regarding themselves as lords. Yes, they are slaves of Satan, their leader, whereas the

SPIRITUAL TREASURES II

13.

A White Rose

This writing uses a rose bush to represent the Holy Trinity, souls, and the road to heaven.

The Lord

Peace be with you my soul!

Soul

My heart is full of joy to hear Your voice again. I thought You had forgot about me. O Lord, I missed You so much. Here I am, Lord, please teach me more about your kingdom. I'm thirsty to hear Your voice and hungry for Your words.

The Lord

My soul, I have a present for you today. I know you always dream of having a rose garden. In that garden you would like to have a white rose.

Soul

Oh, yes, my Lord. So that is why You brought me a white rose bush today. It's so beautiful and I love it. Thanks to you, Lord.

The Lord

My soul, do you want to learn the meaning behind this rose bush?

Soul

Of course, my Lord. Are You going to teach me more about Your kingdom? I would be very honored to learn.

The Lord

My soul, before I tell you anything more about my kingdom, I want you to tell me why you like the roses and why you like the white color more than the other colors.

Soul

Dear Lord, I like roses because they're beautiful. I like the white color because they represent purity.

The Lord

Oh, that's all!?

Soul

Yes, my Lord.

The Lord

My soul, it is more than what you have told me. I will help you to understand a little more about them.

Soul

Please, Lord, please open my mind that I will be able to understand Your word. Please open my eyes that I will be able to see what You see in them.

The Lord

My soul, tell me what you see from them.

Soul

I see the trunk, the thorns around the rose bush, the branches with all the leaves and a few flowers.

The Lord

What else do you see besides the trunk, thorns, branches, leaves and flowers?

Soul

Of course the root, but the root is hidden under the ground.

The Lord

What is that telling you, my soul?

Soul

What do You mean, Lord? It does not mean anything to me.

The Lord

Oh, yes, my soul. It means a lot to you if you listen well to what I'm going to say to you.

Soul

Please, Lord, I can not wait!

The Lord

Every bush must have a root, and from the root, it must have a trunk. From the trunk it must have branches. From the branches it must have leaves and flowers. There are some bushes that give fruits from the flowers.

Now listen well, my soul. The roots, the trunk, and the branches represent the Holy Trinity. The leaves represent the souls, and the flowers represent heaven. The thorns that are around the trunk represent the road to go up to heaven.

Soul

Oh, I think I understand now. The flower's petals are the souls obtaining heaven. They get together as a flower. They pray for the souls who struggle on this earth. The thorns symbolize people who reject You, people who hate You for what You are, people who turn against You or hurt you. So, in order to obtain heaven, I have to learn to accept God's will by being patient, not give in to temptation, and to pray to You, Lord, for the grace to be courageous to pick up the cross and follow You.

The Lord

Well done! I'm very pleased to hear it. You see, that is not difficult, is it?

Soul

Lord, you know better. There is no way that I can do it by myself. You are the Lord, You have given me the grace to do it. Lord, I love you.

The Lord

Come here, my soul *(He held me in His arms with a happy voice.)* You love me! You love me!

Soul

Yes, my Lord. I thank you for all of your blessings toward me. Lord, have mercy on me and my family *(my husband and my son, John)*.

The Lord

(He shook his head and blessed me) Remember, always pray for yourself and for others.

September 8, 1990
Feast of the Birth of the Blessed Mother, Mary

14.

The Conversation with the Lord

People doubt the Lord. Who are the unfortunate? Why we need to say the "Our Father" prayer.

Soul

Lord, I am happy to see You again. I thank you so much for coming.

The Lord

(He shook his head and kept silent.)

Soul

Lord, I am sorry because I know I have hurt You. Will You forgive me?

The Lord

(He is still silent and he moves his leg a little toward me.)

79

Soul

(in the voice of fear) Don't touch me, O Lord. Please don't because I am a sinful person.

The Lord

(He said in a sad voice) I am very sad and lonely.

Soul

(I wonder what he means when he said, "I am very sad and lonely," and how can that be possible? I looked up and saw that His face was still very peaceful but with an expression of sadness.)

The Lord

There are so many people who still doubt me.

Soul

O Lord, I used to doubt You, but not anymore. And now, I love You very much.

The Lord

My soul, I am not talking about you.

Soul

Oh, thank you, Lord. I thought I was the one that hurt You and made You sad. Therefore, I was so fearful. I knew that You loved me much, much more than I loved You. I know now, Lord, that You brought me back from death and gave me life. I mean not only my physical life, but also my spiritual as well. I will always be grateful to You for giving me another chance to come closer to You. Lord, now do you want to share with me the reason for Your loneliness?

The Lord

Yes, my soul *(with an angry voice, He said)* Tell my people to turn away from sin and do not be prideful.

Soul

Lord, please go on and explain to me more.

The Lord

Everything people have comes from my Father. For this reason, people should be humble. They also should not be jealous of their brothers and sisters because this leads to murder. They must love one another as well.

Soul

Lord, may I ask You a question regarding what You just said, "Love one another."

The Lord

(in a gentle voice) What is your question?

Soul

Remember Lord, when I was in bed at the USC hospital, You told me that I would get well and would be a normal person again. Then You said You wanted me to establish a house for the unfortunate. Here I am, I have a heart but no money.

The Lord

(now in a soft voice) My soul, haven't I always given you enough?

Soul

(Somehow, I'm starting to fear Him again. I answered, but shaking) Oh, no. You always have given me enough, but I meant for others.

The Lord

(He is smiling) My soul, if you know I have given you enough, why does it trouble you?

Soul

(I looked at him and felt so guilty. I wanted to cry, but my tears did not come.)

82

The Lord

Whatever you do, you must do within you from the heart. That is most important of all. If you do everything outside, a false heart, then it becomes meaningless. For example, if you have only one dollar left to use and someone comes to your door, and he asks you for money for food, how much will you give to this person? Remember, you only have one dollar.

Soul

That is easy, Lord. What I will do is to give half. He will have 50¢ and I also will have 50¢ to use.

The Lord

My soul, my soul, where is your heart? I want you to think over your decision.

Soul

Lord, then how much should I give to him? Will you tell me?

The Lord

I am not going to make any decision for you or anyone else. You, my soul, you have your own choice. Just like my people, I let them come to me from their own free will. I am not forcing them to do anything that they don't want to do.

Soul

Lord, I think I understand You now. First, You want me to establish in my heart love for all people who are less fortunate than I.

The Lord

Now, my soul, is there any more questions that you want to ask me?

Soul

My question has already been answered by you, Lord. And now I just only want to know what I can tell others about this and how?

The Lord

My soul, tell others that the cross I carried was very, very heavy, because I carried it for all their sins. I want nothing from them but their open heart. I want to live in them and I also want to give them eternal life, not eternal death. Every time they commit sin they offend me. They want to kill me over and over again.

Soul

(I cried when I heard the Lord saying this; therefore I said to Him) Lord, O Lord, You are my God. I have hurt You so much

in the past, but You still forgave me and also have helped me to be protected from eternal death by following Your ways. You have given me a life that no one else can. You also take care of me well and You know my needs. How I was so foolish before. Now I want to continue to live in Your love that You also will live in me. Please Lord, help me to overcome the evil one and please lead me straight.

The Lord

(He held me in His arms about one minute, then He released me.) My soul, I want to show you a miracle.

Soul

(I was so surprised because when the Lord released me, I felt no tears when I wiped them off with my hand) Oh, flood, flood! *(I shouted out loud because the water had come over me and come back out. Oh, that is so beautiful!)*

(I saw I was in front of a big house and it was built out of big square rocks. The house was surrounded with water. Green plants are growing in the water beside the house. I never had seen anything like this before. I just don't have enough words to describe the beauty of it).

The Lord

Jump down into the water and come over here with Me, my soul.

Soul

Lord, I can't swim. How can I come over there with You? Why don't You reach your hand out for me so I can come over?

The Lord

My soul, do not fear! You will be saved when you jump into the water.

Soul

(So I jumped, I was so surprised that the water was not that deep. Under my feet was something very hard. I looked up with an embarrassed smile) I am sorry that I did not trust You earlier when You asked me to jump.

The Lord

My soul, My peace I give you and now you can tell others what you have heard and seen.

Soul

Lord, You are so wonderful. No matter how much I or others hurt You, You still do not condemn us. You still love us and are concerned for us even more. Yes, my Lord, I will carry out Your message in writing.

The Lord

Don't forget to remind others to always give thanks to my Father because everything they receive or they have comes from Him. They should pray more, especially say the "Our Father" prayer. They should at least say it once a day. My Father loves His children when they say it.

Soul

Yes, my Lord, in fact, my heart wants to say it right now.

Our Father, who art in Heaven, hallowed be Thy Name. Thy Kingdom come, Thy Will be done on earth as it is in Heaven. Give us this day our daily bread. Forgive us our trespasses as we forgive those who trespass against us. Lead us not into temptation, but deliver us from evil. Amen.

October 3, 1990
Feast of St. Gerald of Brogne

15.

Forgiveness

This writing uses a dry and wet napkin to explain forgiveness.

The Lord

My soul, what are you doing?

Soul

O Lord, You came back to see me again.

The Lord

Yes, my soul. I am here. I see you're holding some napkins in your hand. I can use this opportunity to give you more wisdom about forgiveness, using the napkins that are in your hand.

Soul

Lord, as You know, I am nothing but dust. This piece of dust is not even worth a penny.

The Lord

But, my soul, this piece of dust is worth a lot in my Father's eyes.

Soul

Dear Lord, if this piece of dust is worth a lot, as You say, then please use it as Your servant.

The Lord

My soul, I will give you knowledge of understanding, which you have seen every day in your life. And when you see this, you will remember what I've taught you. You can then share with others what you learn from me. Now, I want you to bring me two napkins. One that is dry and one that is wet.

Soul

Lord, here are the napkins as You requested, but I still don't understand why You want them.

The Lord

Patience, my soul. Patience.

Soul

Yes, my Lord.

The Lord

Soul, now first I will use a dry napkin to represent those who have a hard time forgiving others. As you see, when your heart is full of hatred, anger, or bitterness toward others, it will become dry like a dry napkin. Do you know why, my soul?

Soul

Dear Lord, please go on and teach me what You mean. I am in darkness and I do need Your help.

The Lord

My soul, I know you would not understand this; therefore, I am here to help you understand things that you don't know.

Soul

Oh, how thoughtful of You, my Lord. How fortunate for me to have You as a teacher. I love You, my Lord.

The Lord

Thank you, my soul. And now, you must listen well. My people actually don't recognize who are their friends and who are their enemies. They are so thoughtless and they will harm themselves in the end.

Soul

Lord, will You tell me who our enemy is?

The Lord

Your enemy is Satan. He tries to tempt my people and my people give in to him. I am the Lord of Peace and the Lord of Mercy. I do no harm to my people.

Soul

Lord, how do I tell if Satan is trying to tempt me?

The Lord

He will try to confuse you. You will feel irritable. This is because you have hatred, anger, or bitterness toward your brothers and sisters. You won't have any peace in your heart. He makes you go against my teachings. That is why you cannot forgive your sisters and your brothers when they do wrong to hurt you.

So, you must stay away from Satan, away from his temptations, and turn to me. Then I can help you to overcome him. See what you should do is to love a person, but hate the evil in him/her. If you can do this, then you find to forgive others is not a difficult thing to do.

Soul

Lord, if I understand correctly, people are hurting one another because they give in to temptation; they hate each other, are bitter or angry toward each other because they listen to Satan, rather than listen to You. Lord, if this is true, then that's terrible.

The Lord

Yes, my soul. It is true. To give in to temptation is a terrible thing for my people to do.

Soul

Lord, is there any way out of this situation?

The Lord

Oh, yes. There is one solution to get out of this trouble.

Soul

Tell me, tell me, Lord.

The Lord

By prayer. If my people turn to me and ask me for help, then I will provide them with the grace they need to overcome. Their hearts will not be so dry like a dry napkin. Their hearts will be soft like a wet napkin.

Soul

Let me think about this. There are so many who have hurt me in the past, why didn't I hate or get angry at them for what they had done to me? Why? I don't understand.

The Lord

Because your tears have wet my feet, yes, my soul; I am the one who gave you the grace to overcome those who hurt you. In fact, I put a shield over you, which protected you. I also gave you the grace to think differently than others when problems come.

Soul

Lord, You have done a lot for me. I feel so ashamed of myself. I know myself well that I am not worthy.

The Lord

Remember, my soul, I know you from inside out. You should be thankful to my Father for the tragedy that will not happen to you.

Soul

Tragedy, what tragedy? Lord, please don't forsake me.

The Lord

The tragedy will happen to those who have a hard heart, a heart so dry like a dry napkin. Because if they won't or can't forgive their brothers or sisters, then my Father also won't forgive them. For example, when they pray to my Father, my Father won't accept their prayer because their prayer is so dry like the heart. Remind my people, don't be dry like a dry napkin, but be soft like a wet napkin.

Soul

Dear Lord, I will give this message to my brothers and sisters.

The Lord

By the way, I want you to know that I wanted to prepare you before my people give you a hard time. So I decided to use the napkins that you are using every day to help you now and also later. Peace, my soul.

Soul

Lord, I so admire You. I can't express my thoughts about You. I am so wordless and speechless before You and Your love toward me. Lord, I love You from the bottom of my heart.

Peace,

A Sinner
October 28, 1990
Feast of St. Jude

16.

An Unexpected Visit

Why we need to say the Holy Rosary often, and pray always.

Soul

(I saw a beautiful lady dressed in blue. Her face was very peaceful and seemed to be white as snow. I asked myself, "Could this person be the Blessed Mother? Oh, I hope that it is." So, I stared at her).

Blessed Mother

Yes, my child.

Soul

Mother! O Mother, it is you. I am so happy to see you. Mother, my eyes . . .

Blessed Mother

Yes, my child, you can see. *(Then She made the sign of the cross on my forehead between my eyes.)*

Soul

Thank you, Mother.

Blessed Mother

(*She shook her head with a smile and said*) Now, my child, what do you see in my hand?

Soul

A rosary, Mother.

Blessed Mother

Yes my child, this is a rosary, which I would like to see all my children have. They should carry a rosary with them because this will protect them from temptation. I also would like to see my children come to me and talk to me more often.

Soul

How, Mother?

Blessed Mother

By prayer. By saying the rosary.

Soul

Yes, Mother.

Blessed Mother

You see, my child, I do not know all of my children. I only know a few who often call on my name for help.

Soul

Mother, please teach me more. Please teach me more, Mother.

Blessed Mother

When you pray, you should not force yourself into it because it is no use to do that. If you have time, say a whole rosary. If you are tired, then say a few because God knows what is in your heart. Be truthful and sincere in your prayer.

Soul

Mother, thank you for reminding me. Mother, I used to fall asleep during my prayers, and when I got up then I continued. Oh, shame on me, Mother, will you please forgive me?

Blessed Mother

(Smiling, she said) I forgive you, my child. And now I have to go.

Soul

Mother, please wait. I would like to know one thing.

Blessed Mother

What is it, my child?

Soul

Mother, why do we have war? And why do people keep hurting one another?

Blessed Mother

The reason for all of this is because people do not pray enough, my child. Pray always, then the world will have peace. Is there any more questions, my child?

Soul

No, Mother. Thank you so very much for being here with me and teaching me. I will do as you have taught me. I will tell others about this, too. Mother, Mother, I love you.

Blessed Mother

Thank you, my child. Before I go, I want to remind you to keep asking the Lord for the things that you need. If He has not answered after your first request, and still not after two, three, four, five times or even more, keep asking. He will give it to you as long as you don't give up hope and if it is of benefit to your soul.

Soul

Thank you, thank you again, Mother. Oh, I love you!

Blessed Mother

Peace now, my child.

Soul

Mother, my heart wants to sing you a song. Then I sang her a song called, "Me Nguon Cay Trong." In English it means, "Mother, Source of Hope.'

Peace.

March 24, 1991
Feast of St. Catherine

17.

Opening Up to the Lord

Words on praying for those who hurt you. Fear God, not mankind. Pray to St. Joseph. The request to establish a prayer group.

Soul

(I am singing Alleluia and folding the clothes at the same time).

The Lord

(in a happy voice) Alleluia! Alleluia! How wonderful! My soul, always remember to sing this song and don't forget to do so.

Soul

Yes, my Lord. O Lord, you are my God. I don't know if I can tell you how I feel about . . . you know what I mean, don't you, Lord?

The Lord

Yes, I think I do, my soul, but I want to hear it from you.

Soul

During one of the semesters of 1980, when I first enrolled in Citrus College, You came and visited me in the office of Mr. Vince O'Boylle, director of the handicapped, in the form of a young man. You were using a wheel chair to get around the campus. There were two ladies who were beside You. The lady on Your right wore a white top and a pair of white pants. The lady on Your left wore a blue top and a pair of black pants. They both had curly hair with the length being above their shoulders.

When You and the two ladies came into the room, You did not say one word to me. You were mute, but the way You looked at me, it was as if You understood my handicap and emotional condition. The lady on Your left did all the talking. Later, before You left Citrus College, You typed on a piece of paper that You wanted me to write to You. I did respond to Your request, but much later.

Then, in 1990, ten years later, I was at a Vietnamese retreat called, "Eucharistic Retreat." My heart was full of joy to see You again without knowing it was the Lord. I just wanted to come to tell You the good news that the Lord had opened my eyes on December 14, 1989 and now I could see again. I also wanted to know if You had received my letter. I looked around for Your wheel chair, and I did not see it anywhere in the room. Then I began to wonder how did You know about this retreat? I did not see any Americans so far at the retreat. Who brought You here? And where were the two ladies who were with You before?

Then I heard You speak, "I am very sad and lonely." I almost clapped my hands and wanted to tell Father An about the second miracle, that The Lord opened Your tongue, because, as You know, You were not able to speak before at Citrus College. But then, I heard someone tell me that this is the Lord, Jesus Christ. I was in shock and said to myself, "The Lord

Jesus Christ. No, how could that be?" Lord, when I realized that it was You, the Lord my God, I just wanted to run and hide from You because I felt so guilty. I now understood not to judge people, because it could be the Lord in disguise.

Somehow Lord, You gave me the courage to kneel down beside You and listen to Your teaching. O Lord, I feel so guilty for my behavior. If I only knew that it was You, I would have responded to You as quickly as I could. But I am still amazed at what You have done for me. I was blind in 1980, but I still could see You well. O Lord, please forgive me. Now, I find out that You are not only my friend, but You are my Lord. So please forgive me, a sinner, Lord.

The Lord

My soul, I forgive you, and I am still your friend.

Soul

Oh, thank you, thank you, Lord. Because only You love me, understand me, and always forgive me when I ask of your forgiveness.

The Lord

My soul, thank you for your appreciation. And, my soul, what do you mean be saying that if you only knew that it was me, then you would treat me different? Why, my soul?

Soul

Oh, dear Lord, I had been brought up in a strict culture and besides, I was hurt by one member of my family. This has been since I was in second grade and until now. I was hurt by so, so many people whom I loved. And so if they knew I write to You, then I would be safe.

The Lord

No, no, my soul. Pray for those who hurt you. And you should not let mankind or culture or anything else stand in your way, especially when you do God's will. My soul, don't fear mankind hurting you, but fear your God.

Soul

Gee! I am so happy to have talked with You and know now that You still love me and come to me. Lord, I also want to thank you for the beautiful gift You gave me in 1980. I did not know then, and I know much more now, that it is You who gives me the ability to help others who are handicapped and are less fortunate than I am. Even though I was blind, I was able to push some of the handicapped to their classes, to the cafeteria, to help them eat their food, to work in the gym. Also, I was able to work on the desk as the receptionist. Oh! Only You can do so many wonderful things.

The Lord

My soul, I just want nothing from you but to do good, to be good, and to continue to ask me for needed graces by prayers.

Soul

Oh, no, Lord! Please don't leave me. Because it is only You that I love. You also love me, don't You, Lord?

The Lord

My soul, I always love you, because I am the Lord of Mercy. My soul, you are ready to face the world again and to do God's will with the abilities that God has given to you.

Soul

Lord, I don't want to be married anymore. May I leave Larry and J.J. and join the Sisterhood to serve you the rest of my life?

The Lord

No, my soul, you may not.

Soul

(I was speechless and also afraid that I might hurt Him. I cried out loud.) I am a sinner, Lord. Please try to understand me and forgive me. It seems like the more I love You, Lord, the more mistakes I make.

The Lord

My soul, you worry too much. I know you try to please me, but if you only knew God already had another plan for you. You don't have to join the Sisterhood in order to serve me.

My soul, there is more than one way to serve your God as long as you have love for your God and your sisters and brothers in My Name. The reason you love them no matter what they are is because they all come from the same tree. This tree is called "God's Tree."

Soul

Thank you, my Lord. How fortunate I am to have You in my life. I can't believe that I feel so close to You now, Lord, because I used to think that You are so far, far away from me and there is no way You know somebody like me, a sinner. So, I always run to Mary, The Mother of God, who happened to be Your mother while You were on the earth. I always call out to Her for help when I don't know whom to turn to.

The Lord

My soul, I am not far away from you or anyone else. I am in everyone's heart. The problem is I know them, but they don't know me. So, my soul, remember to pray for those who do not know me.

Soul

Yes, I will, my Lord.

The Lord

My soul, also do not forget St. Joseph in your prayers. He feels sad because he has been forgotten by people.

Soul

Oh! I don't forget him, Lord, because I don't know any St. Joseph prayer. That is why I don't pray to him.

The Lord

I know that. What is so difficult about saying to him, "St. Joseph, please pray for me?"

Soul

Lord, thank you for helping me. I will pray to him as you have taught me, "St. Joseph, please pray for me."

The Lord

My soul, you make me very happy.

Soul

My Lord, my Lord. You are my God. If You only know how happy I am to hear You say it to me. Lord, I always think that You are not very pleased with me because I always make mistakes with or without my intention.

The Lord

I understand.

Soul

Lord, will You please help me to understand something?

The Lord

What is it, my soul?

Soul

Lord, I have been very emotional lately. I don't know what caused it, but it made my tears pour. So, one day, I brought it up and talked to Father Dai about it.

The Lord

What did Father Dai say to you, my soul?

Soul

Dear Lord, Father Dai said that it is a good sign. This sign means You have touched my heart in the way that I feel so much joy and that is why I cry. He also mentioned that it is very difficult to receive because this is one of God's gifts.

The Lord

My soul, what is there that you don't understand?

Soul

O Lord, You are my God. You might think that I am silly, but I don't know why I have to cry every time You touch me?

The Lord

My soul, my poor soul. If you only knew what God has given you. God doesn't suddenly touch your heart for nothing. My soul, try to remember this; every time God touches your heart, He brings you a special grace. So instead of giving thanks to Him, you question Him for what He has done for you.

Soul

Lord, I don't know why I keep hurting You. Please forgive me again, my Lord.

The Lord

Of course I forgive you. You did not hurt me by asking me a question, which you don't have any knowledge about.

Soul

Thank you again, my Lord. You are really so special. That is why I love you so much.

The Lord

My soul, tell me how many people have come to God and have said thanks to Him for everything that He has given them.

Soul

How many? How many? Lord, I really don't know.

The Lord

(sighs out and says) My soul, there are not very many.

Soul

Lord, I was one of them. I did not know everything I have that came from You, Lord. Now You opened my eyes and gave me the knowledge to understand that without You, I will have nothing. So, that is why I began to give thanks to You for every day of my life. Lord, I hope one day others will get up and realize that without You, they will not have anything.

The Lord

My soul, do not hope, but pray for them.

Soul

Yes, my Lord. Oh, Lord! Oh, Lord! My heart really wants to do something for You, but I am afraid to ask.

The Lord

My soul, what did I tell you earlier? Tell me what is in that mind of yours?

Soul

I would like to have some people get together in Your Name and reach out to others. This program I would call "Anh Sang." In English it means "God of Light." What do you think? Will you approve of this program?

The Lord

Of course I will approve of this program. Remember, if you do everything in My Name, you don't have to wait for my approval unless you do it for your own gain. My soul, what is the purpose of this program?

Soul

Lord, may I sing it to you?

The Lord

That is fine with me, my soul.

Soul

Lay Thay Giesu
la Vua Thien-Dang sinh xuong tran
kho khan khiem nhuong
Vi tinh yeu thuong nhan the
tinh nguyer Vi tha
Doan con Chuong Trinh Anh Sang Thay
Quyet tam vi Chua
Hoc theo guong Chua giang tran
Xin theo got thay
mang duot chan ly yoi khap noi
Hy sinh giup doi
Cong ly nguyer sang nyoi luor
Chien si vi tha
Hang hai dong long cung tier len
Hang Hai luon
So kho chi
the gian ren xiet dau thuong
Cho mong ta tro giup
Tiec chi mot than the rieng

Which in English is:

Dear Lord Jesus Christ,

You who humbly came down to earth, this in thanks to Your endless love. I am willing to form a group that would under the guidance of Your Light be determined to follow Your Light and Truth. We would be willing to sacrifice ourselves to carry to others Your Touch of Truth to enlighten their ways.

Please help this group of "Light" to overcome all difficulties and obstacles in order to be Your soldiers. Also, help us to go forward with courage to carry Your Touch of Truth to the

111

unfortunate who need Your help, our beloved Jesus Christ, our Lord.

The Lord

It is beautiful, my soul. I will send you to Father Dai. He will know what to do. And you, my soul, take good care of Father Dai, can you do that?

Soul

Me, Lord? I can take care of Father Dai, but I . . .

The Lord

My soul, I just want to know if you can or you can not. I don't want to hear the word "but" out of you.

Soul

Yes, my Lord. If You want me to, I will be happy to do it. Because You know my ability better than I.

The Lord

My soul, if you open your heart for me, then I can work. That's all I ask for. Be patient, my soul, then everything will turn out fine.

Soul

My Lord, my Lord, I don't know what to say.

The Lord

My soul, say that you love me and you will always be good.

Soul

Yes, my Lord, I love You and I'll try to be good from now on.

The Lord

Peace, my soul.

LeXuan Tran Koss
July 19, 1991
Feast of St. Arsenius, Monk

18.

Visit from the Lord—His Passion

At a Vietnamese retreat I attended on February 18–20, 1994, the following special event happened.

On the evening of Saturday, February 19, around 11:00 P.M., the priest started to speak about "The Lord's Passion." After he started, I realized in my heart that it was the Lord speaking through him. To the best of my recollection, the following is recorded.

Passion of Our Lord

"My beloved little children. Come here. Please come to me for the Holy Spirit to wash all your sins away. I have seen your hearts and now you are ready for me."

Then the priest sat down on a chair. Then later, the Lord spoke through him again.

"In the Gospel of John and Luke, they wrote about My passion and My rising. In their Gospel, they mention that I had given to My disciples the 'peace' two times. One before My death, and one after I had risen.

"Do you know I am the Lord, but when I was on the earth, I was just like you, except I had no sin. I tell you now, there is only one thing to understand, and that is summarized in only one word, 'Love.' Yes, Lord is Love.

"After supper, I went to the garden and prayed to My Father. I was so terrified. I asked my Father to take away the cup from me. Then one of my veins broke and I sweated blood.

"Then they tied my hands, spit on my face, slapped my face, and they still did not stop there. They played with my beard, and then they pulled my beard. You think they will stop? No, they whipped me and made my skin split and the blood came out and stuck on my garment.

"Do you know what they did next? They took off my garment. I felt so much pain because my blood stuck to my garment, and they kept pulling my garment off my body. I felt like they took a knife and peeled off my skin.

"And they laughed when they put the crown of thorns on my head. At this point, I could not take it any more. I felt that I was so bare in front of them. I wanted to stop, but I thought of you, for example, your name such as Spring, Summer, Autumn, and Winter. And so I asked my Father for the grace of courage to go on.

"Then, they brought me a rough cross and asked me to carry it. Oh, my beloved little children, the cross was so heavy. I was able to take a few steps, then I fell down. One soldier came and kicked me on the side, then two, then ten, twenty, and thirty. They kicked me until I got up again.

"When I got up to the hill, they had me lie on the cross and they tried to pull my hand to the hole, which they already had made for me. My arm was pulled from its socket, my leg was pulled from the hip, and they used a lance to enter into my side to get to my heart. Before I died, I asked my Father to forgive them because they did not know what they were doing.

"And that's why when I had risen from the dead, I asked Thomas to put his hand on my wounds. The most important thing for you is to ask The Holy Spirit for the gift to love your God, the grace of forgiveness, and the gift of courage.

115

"Always remember, if you have any burdens, come to Me and give them to Me. Then I will take them. I want all of you to return to where you were sitting and make yourself comfortable. I am going to give you peace for your heart and peace for your soul."

Then He asked us to say "God is love" three times, then breathe in the air for peace of mind. The Lord then said, "Keep breathing in the air of peace from heaven, the peace for Vietnam, peace for your heart, for your soul, and let it go down to your feet. Breathe in the warm air in the room and let peace take over your body."

Then the Lord left us after the Peace.

Recorded and translated by
LeXuan Tran Koss
February 25–26, 1994

19.

Another Visit from the Lord

Concerns of the author on her life with the Lord.

The Lord

Peace be with you, my loved one!

Soul

My Lord, my God. Is it You?

The Lord

Yes, my loved one. Here I am.

Soul

(in a joyful spirit) Oh, my Lord! I am so happy to talk to You again.

The Lord

So am I my loved one.

Soul

Since You're here, Lord, can I share with You what I have learned?

The Lord

Please tell me what you have learned.

Soul

Lord, do You remember the lesson about the ten fingers? You said to me that ten fingers represent the Ten Commandments, of which the most important commandments are to love your God and to love your neighbor. The two most important commandments are represented by the two thumbs.

The Lord

Yes, my loved one, I do remember.

Soul

Lord, You know I shared this lesson with my Aunty Phan. Do you know what she said?

The Lord

Let me try! Your Aunty Phan said, "Without your two thumbs, you cannot do anything." For example, if you want to pick up a piece of fruit or a book, you cannot do it without your thumbs' help.

My loved one, let me tell you this, a person cannot have anything unless my Father gives it to him. Everything a person has comes from my Father. Therefore, a person must always come to my Father and ask for a need through the "Our Father" prayer. My Father loves to hear His children say this prayer.

Soul

(*Suddenly I began to sing*) "In the dark of the night, I pray to my Lord, have mercy on me. When I look up at the sky, I see many stars shine above. Then I remember Your love for me much, much more than those stars. Oh! My Lord, I beg You to love me and forgive all my mistakes that I have done. Oh! My Lord, at this moment, I put my future life in Your hands." (*I stop and say to myself, "What am I singing?" Then I say to the Lord*) O Lord, You are so wonderful! Thank You for teaching me and helping me to understand much more. O Lord, do You know what I wish? I wish that if You are standing in front of me right now; I could give You a big hug and a big kiss.

The Lord

He laughed and said, "I would give you a big hug and a big kiss, but you would run away and hide yourself inside the blanket."

Soul

(I feel fear of the Lord. I remained quiet for a little while. Then, using all of my courage, I said in a small voice) Lord, when I am face to face with You, I feel like I am naked, filthy, dirty. I feel like You see through me. I am afraid that You would take me and tell everyone how bad I am.

The Lord

(In a soft voice) My loved one, you fear too much. You think I would treat you like others have treated you. You have forgotten I am The Lord, The Lord of love and The Lord of mercy. I understand the human weakness. That is why I am here to give you the purpose that you need. Oh my loved one, if you only knew I have to laugh every time you see me coming and you run to hide inside the blanket.

Soul

Oh, my Lord and my God, I love You. I thought that You wouldn't see me and I would be safe inside my blanket. And You see! And You know it all!

The Lord

Yes, my loved one. I see and I know it all.

Soul

Oh, my Lord, please don't get angry at me and please do not leave me. Lord, please do not hate me for my stupid mistakes.

The Lord

Come now, you don't know better. I love you because you are so innocent and that is why I am here for you.

Soul

Lord, You know I love You because I hurt You the most, but You don't yell at me. You don't scream at me or beat me up like others. You know, Lord, people always think the worst of me. Therefore, when I do something good for someone, I end up in trouble. I am truly sorry to You, Lord, for I had not believed in You for a long time and that's why I did what I did.

The Lord

You may not know me, but your soul knows me.

Soul

May I ask you a question, Lord?

The Lord

Yes, what is it, my loved one?

Soul

How come You don't let others see You? You let me see You and I tell others about You, then they say that I am crazy. I am superstitious. I am telling a lie. I am imagining it, etc. They do not know how much I have changed since You came into my life.

The Lord

They don't see me because they let the material world cover their eyes.

Soul

Lord, since You are here, may I share with You about my concern?

The Lord

What is your concern? I want to hear all about it.

Soul

Dear Lord, sometimes I imagine that I died. My Guardian Angel took me to You. Then You would say to me, "Hi there! Of all my children, You are the one that I show myself to." Then I want You to tell me how much that You have loved me and what You did for me.

Then I answer to You, Lord, "O Lord, I do love You because You are so kind, so loving, and You have forgiven all my mistakes that I have done in the past. Also, You are willing to call me Your friend. And if You ask me how much do I love

You? Then I really cannot say. And if You ask me what I have done for You since then, I also don't know because I do not keep record, but I know this so much. Since You have taught me a lesson, I treat everyone like You have treated me.

Then You ask my Guardian Angel to bring my heart to You. You put my heart on the scale and say, "If your heart is warm, it means you have truly loved Me and if your heart is cold, then you don't have any love for Me at all. This scale not only shows the temperature, it also shows how heavy your heart is. And, if it is heavy, then I know that you love Me and also if you are telling Me the truth. Otherwise, I have nothing to say to you."

O God! I can't go on to imagine anymore. I'm just afraid that You would get angry at me and send me away.

The Lord

(laughed and said) Be happy, my loved one! Just remember my Ten Commandments. Be good! Do good and ask my Father for the graces that you need.

Soul

O God! You know what my heart desires. I always want to make You happy.

The Lord

Oh, my loved one! Don't you think I know what is in your heart and what you are thinking?

Soul

Oh, yes, my Lord! You are my God, and I love You.

The Lord

And now, my loved one. What else do you have concern of?

Soul

About the Cross of Light outside of the bathroom window and the picture of the Mother of Perpetual Help in our front room. Oh, dear God! I told others what I saw, but they did not believe me. This includes the Pastor at St. Louise.

I wrote to the Pastor a report and told him what happened in my home, and so far I hear nothing from him. I would like to have a debate with him on this subject.

Lord, You know I cannot deny You because You have shown me more than others. O Lord, they make me sick because they love to judge when they do not even live in my house and they do not bother to ask for the grace of wisdom. They close their hearts and they close their minds when it comes to You, Lord.

The Lord

Let them be, my loved one. Your job is to pray for them.

Soul

Lord, I am sorry to make You unhappy. I will listen to You. I will pray for them that one of these days they will learn the truth.

The Lord

That is good! Remember what is in the heart counts. And let me take care of the others.

Soul

Yes, my Lord! I love You.

The Lord

(in a happy voice) I love you, too, my loved one. And remember to love me. *(Then His voice changed to sadness.)* LeXuan, although I am happy with my brothers and sisters, I am still sad.

Soul

Why are You sad, my Lord? Is it because of me?

The Lord

Please continue to pray, my loved one. They still do not believe in me. Peace be with you!

Soul

Yes, my Lord, You are my God. You are so wonderful to me. *(Then suddenly I sang to the Lord)* "Oh, my Lord, please love me because I am nobody. Oh, my Lord, please love me because I am a sinner. Alleluia, Alleluia, Alleluia."

LeXuan Tran Koss
April 12, 1996

20.

A Message from the Blessed Mother

Why we need to pray with a humble and sincere heart.

Soul

While I was saying the rosary, I saw a lady in a brown dress that reached to her toes. The cover on her head was also brown. She was holding a small cross on her left arm. I saw tears in her eyes. Her face was white and her lips were very red. I looked at her and wondered, *who is this lady*? It cannot be The Blessed Mother Mary because she looked sad to me.

Blessed Mother

My child! Don't you know me?

Soul

Mother! I cannot believe it is you. Oh, Mother! I am so happy to see you again. But I don't know why you are crying? Am I hurting you, Mother? Please tell me what I have done wrong and please teach me again. I love God much more today than before, and I just want to make God happy.

Blessed Mother

My child, I am crying for my children. *(Then she pointed at her eyes and said)* See, my child.

Soul

Mother Mary! Please teach me.

Blessed Mother

They have sinned against God. They don't pray any more. They don't please God any more. They live so much with their flesh. Do you know what, my child? God, the Father, is very angry and He is getting ready to destroy the world that He has created.

Soul

Mother Mary, I really don't understand when you said people don't pray anymore. From what I know, there are many prayer groups.

Blessed Mother

Come!

Soul

I don't know how to explain it, but when the Blessed Mother said the word "Come," I then saw myself kneeling beside her.

She sat down on the chair. I knelt down on her right. Next to her, on the left, there also was a chair. I didn't see a body, but only two hands.

Blessed Mother

(*pointed in front of her and said*) My child, let's see now.

Soul

I saw a few red roses with long stems. They were slowly coming up in front of the Blessed Mother. She took them and gave them to the hands next to her. As she gave the roses to the hands, the roses quickly disappeared.

I counted the roses. There were five roses that Mother Mary received.

Now I understand. Even though there are so many people in prayer groups, there are very few of those people whose prayers are accepted by God. I bowed my head on the ground and said, "Please forgive me. I didn't know you then, but I know you now."

Blessed Mother

Get up, my child! God has seen your heart.

Soul

Thank you, Mother Mary! And then I found myself back where I was before, lying on my bed.

Blessed Mother

Now, my child, please tell me why you are lying in bed and what are the tears for?

Soul

Mother Mary, I feel hurt because of others' attitude towards me. I just don't feel like I want to go on with my life anymore.

Blessed Mother

I know you are hurting; that is why I am here. I want you to think that you're learning how to walk. And, of course, I always will be there for you and pick you up when you fall down.

Soul

Mother Mary, I don't think that I can go on.

Blessed Mother

My child, look over there! You see, Jesus is waiting for you.

Soul

I looked up and I saw a man with a long white robe. He opened his arms like he was waiting to hold me in his arms. I could not see his face well because his face was so white and so bright.

Blessed Mother

My child, now you know why you cannot give up. You must learn to be like a child. If you fall down, then you have to try to get up again.

Soul

Mother Mary, thank you for being here to help me out. Just sometimes I feel like I am so dumb. I just don't know any other prayers than Our Father, Hail Mary and the Glory Be, and others always know what to say to the Lord.

Blessed Mother

(*smiled and said*) My child, what are you saying? Remember the five roses that you just saw? They are also as dumb as you are. They don't know how to use fancy words when they pray. Their prayers are so simple and with a humble heart. Therefore, God accepted their prayers. So, be happy, my child!

Soul

Mother Mary, I am feeling better now because it is okay to be dumb. Thank you so much, Mother. I love you!

Blessed Mother

Remember, my child, be happy! Don't worry! Peace and love to you.

Soul

I love you, Mother Mary. Please help me to be a better person every day in my life. *(I continued to finish my rosary and hoped my prayer will be accepted by God.)*

LeXuan Tran Koss
June 30, 1996

21.

I Am Now One with the Lord

The following is my reflection on the Word of God as it relates to my life.

This people honors me with their lips, but their heart is far from me [MK 7:6].

My early childhood, ages three to ten, to my knowledge, were the worst years of my life. My relationship with God, during that time, was physical, from my lips, not from my heart. I was angry with God and filled with hatred toward Him. This was because I didn't know what I had done so wrong to have God hate me so bad. He allowed the people around me to hurt me physically and mentally. This continued until I was thirty-one years old.

As I remember correctly, I was sick during my senior year in high school. This sickness carried through my senior year until I graduated from Gladstone High School. I ended up in USC/Los Angeles County Hospital on July 4, 1978. I was unconscious about three months with cryptococcal meningitis. Even though I was unconscious, I knew what was going on because I saw the people who came to see me and heard what they said to me. However, I was not able to talk back to the people who came to my bed to visit me.

During that time, I heard one of the people who visited me say, "God punished her and He made her this way." When

I heard this, I felt very sad and wondered, *Who is God and why did He punish me?* Then one day, I saw a Catholic priest was beside my bed. I saw that he looked at me, and I wanted to know from him why God punished me? Why did God hate me? Why did God love everyone else but me? With all these thoughts in my mind, I was not able to ask. Father blessed me and prayed over me. Then he said to someone in the room, "I don't know if she is a Catholic or not. I gave her the Last Rites, just in case." I heard no response after the priest made his comments.

I asked myself, "What is it? What is the Last Rites? What is the priest doing to me now?"

After three months, I regained consciousness. I still was not able to communicate well. I had a speech problem. On top of that, I had lost my eyesight. I asked the nurse if she could take me to church. She said yes, but it never happened. Then I asked to see a priest, but the hospital didn't provide me with one. Through my family, however, my father brought a Vietnamese priest a few times to see me. His name was Reverend Father James Phan Van Dai, now deceased. He brought to me the Holy Eucharist without talking with me. This caused me a lot of sadness and feeling of rejection.

During the time I was in the hospital, I felt as if I wanted something inside of me, but I did not receive it. I was not hungry physically, but every day I felt hungry for something. I did not know what I wanted exactly. So then I refused to eat, to drink, and to take my medication. I wanted to die. I became depressed because there was nobody to understand me. Every time they came to visit me, they just yelled at me. Why did I not talk to them? The nurses saw I cried every day and did not want to eat or drink, or even take my medication. They took me to see another patient. They told me, "If you continue what you are doing now, we will have to put a tube in you just like that man over there." It did not matter to me, I just wanted to

134

meet God and wanted to know why He punished me this way and what I did to Him?

So I began to wish that my parents would move to live close to the church, so that I could go to church and find Him. And yet, while I was in the hospital bed, my parents told me that they had found a house close to church within walking distance. I was happy when I heard the news and looked forward to going home so that I could go back to church to find God. Then when the doctor came to check on me, my question to him was always, "May I go home please?"

One day, one of the doctors asked me to walk. This was because he wanted to check my balance. He shook his head and said, "Your walking is unsteady. You can't go home yet." This made me cry more and more every day. They finally had enough of my crying and they decided for me to be an outpatient of the hospital after almost one year in the hospital.

While I stayed at home as an outpatient, I was able to go to church with one of my sisters on Sunday. Then one day, I decided to go to church myself, with the hope that God would tell me why He hated me. Every day I went to church and asked Him, "If you are truly God, then please come down from the Cross and talk to me. I just want to know why are you punishing me this way and what I have done to You?" I heard no response and I thought God was not in the church.

So I went and looked for Him in a convent of the Dominican Sisters. I did not find Him there. Then I thought that God hated me so bad at this point He did not want to speak to me. This made me angrier because I felt that God looked at me as a bad person by taking away my eyesight and by having cryptococcal meningitis. It was on February 25, 1990 that The Lord Jesus Christ revealed to me who He was when He first appeared to me sometime in February 1980.

In February 1980, while I was attending Citrus College as a blind, handicapped student, the following event happened. I didn't know who Jesus was when He was comforting me in the appearance of a young man in a wheel chair and was mute. He would use a typewriter to communicate to me. A lady would then read aloud what he typed because being blind I couldn't read. During the encounter with the young man, He said to me, "Be happy! Even though I am sad, when I am with my brothers and sisters, I am happy." My response to Him, at that time was, "It is easy for you to say. You do not know how I feel inside. Do you think I want to be sad?" He responded, "Write to me!" Because of my Vietnamese culture, which doesn't permit a girl to write to a boy first, I didn't write to him for a year. Still being blind, I took the courage to ask Diana Russo of my Junior College Handicapped Center to write a formal letter to the young man, at his request. She helped me to write a formal letter to him. We sent it to another junior college, Mount San Antonio. Then I was fearful of my parents knowing that I wrote a letter to a young man. Therefore I wished the young man did not send the letter back to me.

Ten years later, while I was attending a spiritual retreat, February 24–26, 1990, the Lord revealed Himself to me. I saw exactly the young man that I had met once in the Citrus College Handicapped Center. He had on exactly the clothes that He wore before. The only thing that I did not see was his wheel chair, as well as the two young women who were with him then. I wondered how he knew about the Vietnamese Retreat and how he got here? I did not see him the night before.

My heart was full of joy. I could not wait to tell Him the good news that I was able to see a little. At the same time, I wondered if He ever received my letter. All kinds of things I wanted to share with Him, but I could not do it yet. I had to wait for Father, the retreat leader, to finish his talk.

Then I heard Him say in Vietnamese, "I am very sad and lonely!" And again my heart jumped with joy. I said to myself,

"He speaks Vietnamese!" Then I almost ran to Him to ask Him to say together thanks be to God, because He was able to speak, and I was able to see a little. Even though I was not able to see a lot, it meant a lot to me. Then I heard a girl say to another girl, "Who is that young man?" The response was it was the Lord Jesus Christ.

When I heard this, I ran to the kitchen, where I ran into my uncle. He asked me, "Where were you going?" I said, "I was looking for my sister, I want to go home." He said, "Your sister is still in there." I asked him, "What was wrong in there?" He said, "Go back in there and ask Jesus what is wrong?" I asked my uncle, "Do you want me to ask?" Then I ran out of the back door to the parking lot frightened. Somehow I ended up in the retreat room.

I then saw the Blessed Mother at the door, dressed in blue, with two girls holding her hands. She looked at me, and I looked at her. Then I saw Jesus standing in the middle of the room. I asked myself this question, "Whom should I come to first?" Should I run to Jesus and ask Him why He hated me and why He was continually punishing me? Or should I come to the Blessed Mother, whom I did love. Then I decided I would go to Jesus because I wanted to know why did He hate me and why did He punish me. So then I ran to Jesus.

He looked at me. Then He asked me with love and a gentle voice, "What gift do you want of Me?" I was trembling, kneeled down, and responded, "I want to get to know You, to learn to love You, and to serve You through Your people." Then He said, "Bring to me the Cross." Somehow I saw Him hold in His arm the cross against His heart. He then asked me, "Do you want anything else of me?" "Yes," I responded. "Will you please tell my family that I was innocent all this time." He said, "You are not perfect yet. Come to Me so I can give."

I then trembled again, and He asked me to say the "Our Father" prayer. I said it and He asked me to say it again. Then

I said it again. At this point He asked me to say it with Him, and I did. I recognized my mistakes when I was saying the words of the prayer. Then He said, "I wanted you to remember God the Father likes to hear His children say this prayer." Then He went to a young man not too far away from me. He knelt down in front of the young man and said, "Open your heart for Me to come in." The man knelt there and didn't do anything. Jesus pleaded to him, "Please open your heart for me to come in." The man still didn't react. Jesus' face saddened. He pleaded again to the young man, "Open your heart, open your heart, please open it so I can come in." The man still didn't move.

Then I saw the Blessed Mother in blue, whom I saw earlier, come to this young man. It seemed Jesus had left, but His presence was felt strongly, He was still there. She then placed her hand on his chest and rubbed it gently. As she rubbed she said, "Jesus loves you. Open your heart for Him. Please open your heart." When I saw and heard it, my head bowed down touching the floor. Then I said to Jesus, "I am so sorry. I did not know you then, but I know you now. Please forgive me."

I then heard a man's voice call my name. I looked up and I didn't see anyone in the room except for the priest and me. I was not able to understand, and I kept looking around in the room. The priest said to me, "Everyone has gone to sleep. I suggest you do the same." When I got up to go, I realized that I felt peace in my heart, even though I was not able to understand what was happening to me. The priest then asked me, "Did you experience something tonight?" I did not know how to tell the priest and so looked at the priest and walked out of the room.

Over a year later in May 1991, starting on my birthday and then my son John's, I began to ask Jesus to give me a house that I can use as a prayer house, and the Lord Jesus Christ will send people to come and pray with me. The reason I asked

Him to choose the people is that I don't know how to pray. I also didn't know how to say the Rosary. Within a short period of time, Jesus gave us a home of our own as I requested.

We moved in the last week of August 1992. In January 1993, a Cross of Light appeared in our bathroom window facing our front yard. Then in April 1993, on Good Friday, the Lord of Light Prayer Group was formed. On that Good Friday, a new prayer was learned from Julie, Mary Ann, and Irene. It was "O Jesus, I believe, I adore, I hope and I love You. And I ask your pardon for all those who do not believe, who do not adore, who do not hope and do not love you." I kept saying this prayer over and over again, and every time I said it, my tears kept on rolling down on my cheek. I felt I was not only asking God to forgive me, but I was afraid for others. This was because I now know there is really a True God. He is a loving God and merciful God and He died for my sins. Today I learned:

1. I used to run around looking for Jesus. Now I know He always is in my heart.
2. That when I go to confession, I just don't go to tell the priest what I think the priest wants to hear, how bad I am. Now I would be more truly sorry for my actions, in my words, and also for my thoughts that I had sinned against God.
3. Jesus is not only in the confessional, He is also in the Tabernacle.
4. When the priest offers the Eucharist, he changes bread and wine into the Body and Blood of Our Lord Jesus Christ, present as the True God Himself.
5. I used to think that only the Words of God were the most important part of the whole Mass. Now I have learned the whole Mass is important. Not only do we hear God's Words and receive Him in the Eucharist, we satisfy the four obligations we owe to God: 1) to give Him honor, praise and

glory; 2) to ask for His Mercy, to forgive my sins; 3) to thank Him for His gifts; and 4) to ask Him for what I need.

6. I used to believe that I wasn't receiving Jesus when the priest said "Body of Christ." I thought the priest tried to scare me. Now I believe Jesus is God and when I receive Him, the Host, and drink the wine, I truly receive His Body and Blood.

7. I knew only one Mother Mary, as the Mother of Perpetual Help. If I would see her in other forms, I was not able to tell who she was, especially when I saw her without Jesus.

8. I did not relate Mother Mary as the mother of Jesus. Now I do.

9. I did not know Jesus is my brother. Now I do.

10. I did not know Jesus died for my sins. I thought He committed a terrible sin, which I could not figure out. What was it that He had committed? Now I know He committed the gift of love. He loves me so much and that is why He is on the Cross for me.

My point is if you don't know God like I did in my early age, how do you come to God and be one with Him? Even though I know God today, I still don't understand if God, Jesus Christ, is the head, and we are members of His Body. This to me means we become brothers and sisters in Christ. Why then can we not be able to love one another, and be kind or be nice to one another? I will never be able to understand. I just know this much for myself. I must love God and must love my brothers and sisters. I try to show God how much I love Him through my actions and my words toward my brothers and my sisters. And when I pray, I pray from my heart, not from my lips. Everything I do, I do out of love for the Lord.

Since August 27, 2000, I felt like I started my life all over again. This is because in my new life, I acknowledge that God is in me, and I am in Him. My heart desires to receive Him.

This is in order to be filled of my need. I am able to go to daily Mass and able to say the Rosary with others, because I still cannot say the Rosary by myself. It takes me one hour to walk home from the daily Mass, but at least I have filled my hunger.

O Lord, thank you for giving me the gift of yourself. Please do not take it away from me. I don't mind if I have to walk an hour to receive Your flesh, as long as You fill me with my need. O Lord, I am so hungry for You and so thirsty for Your Word. Oh, please Lord, love me and don't take it away like other humans do. Thank you again, my Lord, for your love for me. O Mother Mary, please pray for me and walk with me. Please guide me to your son, Jesus. Oh, my Jesus, I adore You and I love You. O Mother Mary, you know my need. Mother, I love you and please pray for me. Amen.

September 15, 2000
Feast of Lady of Sorrows